Hello, Family Members,

Learning to read is one of the mosnts of early childhood. **Hello Reader** elp children become skilled readers ing readers learn to read by rememl rds like "the," "is," and "and"; by using _____ new words; and by interpreting picture and text clues. These books provide both the stories children enjoy and the structure they need to read fluently and independently. Here are suggestions for helping your child *before*, *during*, and *after* reading:

Before
- Look at the cover and pictures and have your child predict what the story is about.
- Read the story to your child.
- Encourage your child to chime in with familiar words and phrases.
- Echo read with your child by reading a line first and having your child read it after you do.

During
- Have your child think about a word he or she does not recognize right away. Provide hints such as "Let's see if we know the sounds" and "Have we read other words like this one?"
- Encourage your child to use phonics skills to sound out new words.
- Provide the word for your child when more assistance is needed so that he or she does not struggle and the experience of reading with you is a positive one.
- Encourage your child to have fun by reading with a lot of expression . . . like an actor!

After
- Have your child keep lists of interesting and favorite words.
- Encourage your child to read the books over and over again. Have him or her read to brothers, sisters, grandparents, and even teddy bears. Repeated readings develop confidence in young readers.
- Talk about the stories. Ask and answer questions. Share ideas about the funniest and most interesting characters and events in the stories.

I do hope that you and your child enjoy this book.

—Francie Alexander
Reading Specialist,
Scholastic's Learning Ventures

For Keith, with all my love
— K.W.

To Laurie McFarlin,
Thanks for sending me to school.
— P.S.

Text copyright © 2001 by Kimberly Weinberger.
Illustrations copyright © 2001 by Portia Sloan.
All rights reserved. Published by Scholastic Inc.
SCHOLASTIC, HELLO READER, CARTWHEEL BOOKS, and associated logos
are trademarks and/or registered trademarks of Scholastic Inc.

Library of Congress Cataloging-in-Publication Data

Weinberger, Kimberly.
    Mummies unwrapped / by Kimberly Weinberger; illustrated by Portia Sloan.
        p.   cm.—(Hello reader! Level 3)
    ISBN 0-439-20058-X
    1. Mummies—Juvenile literature. [I. Mummies. 2. Egypt—Antiquities.] I. Sloan,
Portia, ill. II. Title. III. Series

GN293 .W45 2001
393'.3—dc21   00-029699

        12 11 10 9 8 7 6 5 4 3   02 03 04 05 06

                        Printed in the U.S.A.   24
                        First printing, April 2001

·MUMMIES·
UNWRAPPED!

BY KIMBERLY WEINBERGER
ILLUSTRATED BY PORTIA SLOAN

Hello Reader! — Level 3

SCHOLASTIC INC.

New York   Toronto   London   Auckland   Sydney
Mexico City   New Delhi   Hong Kong

◇ CHAPTER ONE ◇
TO LIVE FOREVER

They lived thousands of years ago.
They prayed to many gods and goddesses.
They built great temples and tombs.
They are the ancient Egyptians.

The Egyptians believed that each person
was born with an invisible twin called
the *ka*.
This twin lived on after the person died,
staying close to the body forever.
The *ba*, or soul of a person, also survived.
It flew away from the body after death.

For the dead person to live in the Next
World, its ba must be able to return to it.
But the ba had to know which was the
right body.
The Egyptians worried that this was
not always possible.

Early Egyptians buried their dead in holes in the sand.

There, the hot, dry weather kept the bodies from rotting.

But soon the wealthy began burying their loved ones in stone tombs.

They then made a horrible discovery. Without the desert sands, the bodies quickly became skeletons!

The ba would never be able to tell one body from another.

Without the ba, the dead person was lost forever.

Now these wealthy Egyptians were faced with a problem.

They wanted to honor their dead with beautiful tombs.

But they also had to keep the bodies from rotting away.

The desert sands had taught them that the body could be saved if kept dry.

After many years, the Egyptians found the perfect way to save, or preserve, themselves.

They began a fascinating practice—the making of mummies.

This worked so well, in fact, that some of their bodies are still around today!

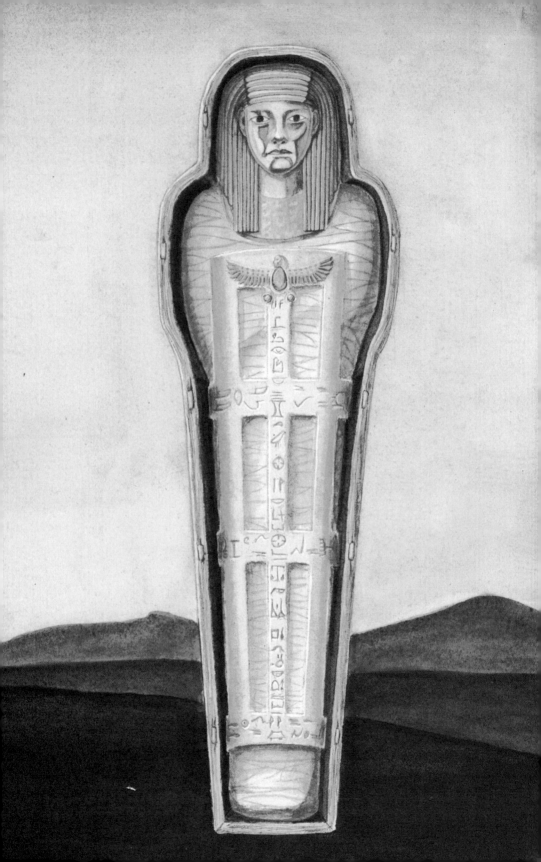

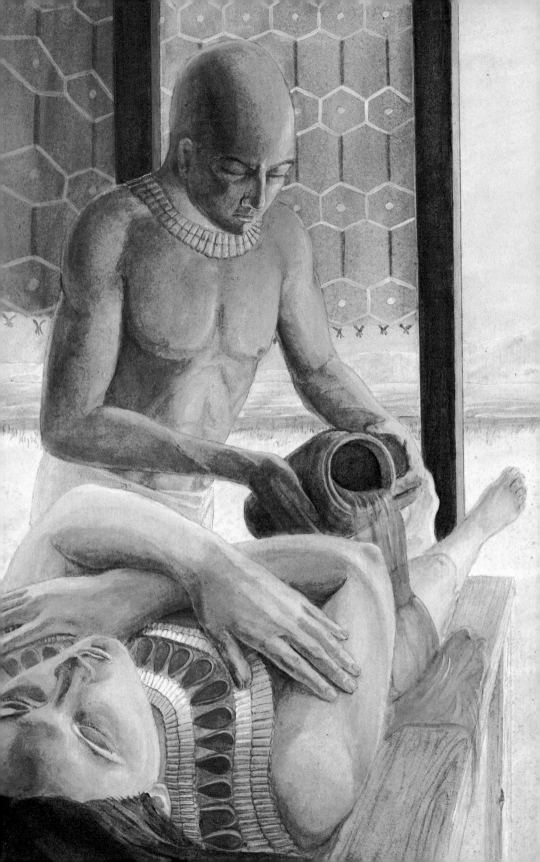

◇ CHAPTER TWO ◇
TO MAKE A MUMMY

When an Egyptian died, the body was taken to a tent called the *ibu,* the Place of Washing.

There the body was washed with wine and rinsed with water from the great Nile River.

The men who did this work were called *embalmers.*

Next the body was moved to the
embalmers' workshop.
The liver, lungs, stomach, and intestines
were all removed.
They were dried using a natural salt
called *natron*.

Then they were placed in *canopic jars*. These were special holders with lids in the shape of human or animal heads.

The heart of the dead person
was left in the body.
The Egyptians believed that the heart
was the center of reason and feeling.
The dead person would need it on the
trip to the Next World.
The brain, though, was not thought to be
important at all!

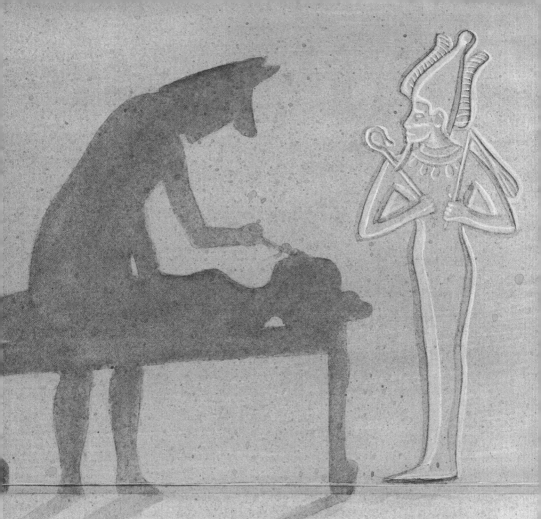

It was thrown away after embalmers
used a long hook to pull it out through
the nose.

They then stuffed and covered the body
with natron.

After 40 days, the body was completely
dried out.

Once dry, the body was washed again with water.

Oils were rubbed into the skin to make it softer.

Cloth scented with spices was stuffed inside the head and body.

The cut made to remove the body's insides was sewn up.

Beautiful jewelry was added.

Then it was time to begin wrapping.

The embalmers used fine, thin linen cloth.
First they wrapped the head and neck,
then each finger and toe.
Next came the arms and legs, and finally
the body.

As the body was wrapped, priests
sang spells.
These spells would protect the mummy
on its trip to the Next World.
Crocodiles, snakes, and even evil gods
would make the journey very dangerous.
Charms called *amulets* were placed
between the layers of linen for protection.
A glue called *resin* held the linen together.
The last step was to place a painted mask
on the mummy.

From start to finish, it took 70 days to make one mummy.

Because of the many workers needed, only the wealthy could afford to be so well preserved.

And who was the wealthiest person in Egypt?

The great and mighty king, of course— also known as the *pharaoh*.

◇ CHAPTER THREE ◇
TO RULE THE LAND

Pharaohs were believed to be half-human and half-god.

When a pharaoh died, he was given a very grand funeral.

He would join the gods in the Next World in the *Field of Reeds*.

Life in the Field of Reeds was thought
to be wonderful.
There was plenty of food and drink.
A great river flowed through the land.
The dead, now healthy and happy, lived
in peace.
This world was ruled by a god named
Osiris.

Egyptians believed that the god Osiris
was once Pharaoh of Egypt.
He was wise and good, and all of Egypt
loved him.
But Osiris had an evil and jealous brother
named *Seth.*
To take over the throne of Egypt, Seth
killed Osiris.

Soon after Osiris died, his wife, *Isis,* gave birth to his son and named him *Horus.*

While Osiris ruled the Land of the Dead, his son, Horus, took Egypt back from the evil Seth.

As ruler of the Field of Reeds, Osiris
judged all who hoped to enter.
A dead person's heart was weighed on a
scale against a feather.

If the heart was light and free of sin, the scales balanced.

The person went on to the Field of Reeds.

But if the heart was evil, it was fed to *Ammit*, "the Eater of the Dead."

The person would be lost forever.

Ammit was a monster with the head of a crocodile.

It had front legs like a lion and back legs like a hippopotamus!

To get to the Field of Reeds safely, the dead were helped by the living.
A prayer called the *Opening of the Mouth* allowed the dead to speak and eat again. Priests sang more spells to protect them.

Coffins were painted with magical words
and pictures.
Large tombs were built.
Of course, pharaohs received the
finest coffins and tombs.

Early royal tombs were called *mastabas*.
A room was dug deep in the ground to
house the body.
Above ground, walls of mud and brick
ended in a flat roof.

Later, pharaohs built great *pyramid tombs*.

Still later, tombs were hidden in the rocky walls of deserted valleys.

Though Egyptians worked hard to keep them safe, few mummies were able to rest in peace.

Danger was waiting, sometimes as soon as the funeral ended.

What was this danger?

Robbers!

◇ CHAPTER FOUR ◇
TO FIND THE TREASURE

Tombs of the very wealthy were filled with goods.

Anything the dead person might need in the Next World was there.

The dead were given furniture, clothes, food, and weapons.

There were even small statues of servants called *shabtis*.

Egyptians believed the shabtis would come to life in the Next World to serve the dead.

Paintings of food and drink on the tomb walls were also thought to become real.

Above all, every wealthy tomb had one thing in common—gold.

Robbers would risk their lives to find a
tomb's treasure.
They would search through dark, secret
hallways laid with dangerous traps.
Falling into hidden pits or deep wells
would mean instant death.
But stealing the mummy's gold and jewels
meant even more.
Sadly, most robbers were successful.
Very few tombs stayed hidden from them.
But one tomb did.
And it captured the attention of the world
more than 3,000 years later.

In 1922, a man named Howard Carter found the entrance to a tomb in Egypt. It belonged to a young pharaoh named *Tutankhamen*.
Inside were golden statues and shining jewels.
Though robbers had stolen some things, most of the treasure remained.

But where was Tutankhamen's mummy?
Slowly and carefully, Carter worked his
way through the rooms of the tomb.
Finally, three years later, he arrived at the
burial chamber.
There, three golden coffins sat, one
inside another.
In the smallest coffin, King Tutankhamen
was found.

Tutankhamen, also known as King Tut, is probably the world's most famous mummy.
But he was not a very important pharaoh in the history of Egypt.
We can only wonder what riches might have been buried with the greatest pharaohs of the land.
Perhaps one day we'll find out!